Praise for the Believe Series

"As grandparents of fifty grandchildren, we heartily endorse the *Believe and You're There* series. Parents and grandparents, gather your children around you and discover the scriptures again as they come alive in the *Believe and You're There* series."

—STEPHEN AND SANDRA COVEY
Stephen Covey is the bestselling author of *7 Habits of Highly Effective People*

"Bravo! This series is a treasure! You pray that your children will fall in love with and get lost in the scriptures just as they are discovering the wonder of reading. This series does it. Two thumbs way, way up!"

—MACK AND REBECCA WILBERG
Mack Wilberg is the music director of the Mormon Tabernacle Choir

"This series is a powerful tool for helping children learn to liken the scriptures to themselves. Helping children experience the scriptural stories from their point of view is genius."

—ED AND PATRICIA PINEGAR
Ed Pinegar is the bestselling author of *Raising the Bar*

"We only wish these wonderful books had been available when we were raising our own children. How we look forward to sharing them with all our grandchildren!"

—STEPHEN AND JANET ROBINSON
Stephen Robinson is the bestselling author of *Believing Christ*

"The *Believe and You're There* series taps into the popular genre of fantasy and imagination in a wonderful way. Today's children will be drawn into the reality of events described in the scriptures. Ever true to the scriptural accounts, the authors have crafted delightful stories that will surely awaken children's vivid imaginations while teaching truths that will often sound familiar."

—TRUMAN AND ANN MADSEN
Truman Madsen is the bestselling author of *Joseph Smith, the Prophet*

"My dad and I read *At the Miracles of Jesus* together. First I'd read a chapter, and then he would. Now we're reading the next book. He says he feels the Spirit when we read. So do I."

—CASEY J., age 9

"My mom likes me to read before bed. I used to hate it, but the *Believe* books make reading fun and exciting. And they make you feel good inside, too."

—KADEN T., age 10

"Reading the *Believe* series with my tweens and my teens has been a big spiritual boost in our home—even for me! It always leaves me peaceful and more certain about what I believe."

—GLADYS A., age 43

"I love how Katie, Matthew, and Peter are connected to each other and to their grandma. These stories link children to their families, their ancestors, and on to the Savior. I heartily recommend them for any child, parent, or grandparent."

—ANNE S., age 50
Mother of ten, grandmother of nine (and counting)

When Daniel
Was Delivered

Books in the *Believe and You're There* series

Believe and You're There

When Daniel
Was Delivered

Book 10

ALICE W. JOHNSON & ALLISON H. WARNER

DESERET BOOK

Salt Lake City, Utah

Visit us at DeseretBook.com

Library of Congress Cataloging-in-Publication Data

Johnson, Alice W.
  Believe and you're there when Daniel was delivered / Alice W. Johnson and Allison H. Warner ; illustrated by Casey Nelson.
      p. cm.
  Summary: Katie, Matthew, and Peter travel through their grandma's painting to the time of Daniel. As they anxiously await to see what happens when Daniel is thrown into the lion's den, they learn the importance of being loyal to God, even when others don't understand.
  ISBN 978-1-60641-817-8 (paperbound)
  1. Daniel (Biblical figure)—Juvenile literature. 2. Bible stories, English.
I. Warner, Allison H. II. Nelson, Casey (Casey Shane), 1973– ill.
III. Title.
  BS580.D2J64 2010
  224'.509505—dc22   2010024122

Printed in the United States of America   10/2010
R. R. Donnelley, Crawfordsville, IN

10   9   8   7   6   5   4   3   2   1

Believe in the wonder,
Believe if you dare,
Believe in your heart,
Just believe . . . and you're there!

Contents

Chapter One

A Middle School Mess

The soft sun of summer's end streamed through the red and yellow leaves on the trees in front of Grandma's house. Autumn had officially arrived, and Katie, Matthew, and Peter were busily raking the colorful leaves that had already fallen all over their grandma's front lawn.

"You're running for student council?" Katie asked, surprised by her younger brother Matthew's announcement that he was running for office at the local middle school.

"Wow! I'm really proud of you," Peter, age nine, said admiringly. He looked up to his older brother and was always proud to claim their relationship. "My friends will be really impressed when I tell them my big brother is an officer on the student council."

"Whoa, little buddy. Remember, I'm not on it yet. I still have to run for office *and* win the election. That's not going to be easy, you know." Matthew smiled as he tousled Peter's unruly mop of red-brown curls.

"Have you written your speech for the school assembly yet?" Katie asked. "I'd love to help you."

"Thanks, Sis, but I'm not going to give an actual speech," Matthew replied. "We've decided I should play my guitar and sing, instead."

"Who is *we*?" Katie asked.

"Brad and Jason. They're the ones who talked me into running, and they're going to help me get elected," Matthew said.

"I didn't know you were good friends with *them*," Peter said, a hint of doubt in his voice.

"What's wrong with *them*?" Suddenly, Matthew was on the defensive.

"I didn't say there was anything *wrong* with them. They just don't seem like your type, that's all," Peter answered innocently, as he dragged a big sack full of leaves to the curb.

Katie eyed Matthew carefully. This defensive tone was not like him at all. *What's up with Matthew?* she thought to herself as she raked the last of the leaves into a pile.

"I mean, Brad and Jason may dress a little radical, and they may talk a little rough, but that doesn't mean they're not good guys," Matthew said, trying to explain.

"Okay, if you say so," Peter muttered, raising his eyebrows as he ran and jumped into the middle of the leaf pile.

Matthew glared at Peter. Katie quickly intervened, trying to calm Matthew's ruffled feathers. "What are you planning to sing at the assembly?" she asked Matthew.

"Brad and Jason have written a song for me. They say it's really cool," Matthew said. "Here's the jacket they're letting me borrow to wear when I sing."

Matthew pulled from his backpack a heavy black leather jacket with a white skull and crossbones painted on the back.

Peter looked horrified. "That's something a tough fighter guy in a gang would wear!"

"How would you know?" Matthew shot back. "Have you ever seen a gang member?"

"Well, not in real life . . . ," Peter admitted as he stood up and brushed the leaves off his sleeves.

"Okay, then, so you don't really know," Matthew spoke sharply, and returned to raking with determination.

Before Peter could reply, Katie stepped in to cool things down. "I've never seen a real gang member, either," she said, holding a bag open for Matthew to fill with leaves. "But, Matthew, do you really want to wear a jacket that makes you look rebellious and mean?"

"It's just this one time," Matthew told his sister, not looking her in the eye.

"I see . . . ," Katie answered, thinking of what she ought to say next. "Tell me about this song," she said, changing the subject, as she picked the last of the leaves out of Peter's hair.

"Brad and Jason have made up new words to a song by the Grunge Worms," Matthew explained, trying to sound like it was no big deal.

"You are going to wear *that* jacket and sing a Grunge Worm song?" Peter couldn't believe what he was hearing. "Your guitar can't even make that hard rock sound!"

"I know that! I'm going to play Jason's

electric guitar," Matthew said, his voice still defensive.

"That doesn't sound like you at all," Katie said.

"I know. That's the neat thing about it. Brad and Jason say that everyone thinks I'm a little goody-goody, so this will really get people's attention. And then I'll get more votes," Matthew said in a half-hearted attempt to explain himself. "That's what Brad and Jason say, anyway."

"I hope no one remembers that you're my brother," Peter said quietly, almost under his breath.

"What do you mean by that?" Matthew asked, clearly stung by Peter's words. Matthew had always tried to be a good example to his younger brother, and it made him happy that Peter looked up to him.

"Just what I said." Peter was forthright and unapologetic. "I hope no one realizes you are my brother. I tell all my friends how great you are, and that you always stand up for what you believe. You wouldn't *normally* act this way, so why act this way *now*?"

In response, Matthew hung his head. He felt

pulled in so many directions. He wanted to be on the student council, and he wanted to win the approval of his friends. And popular Brad and Jason seemed so confident about their campaign plans. But Matthew couldn't stand to disappoint his little brother either. What was he going to do?

"I guess I agreed to their campaign ideas because I really want to get elected," Matthew said, sounding deflated.

"Well, I think people would want to vote for the *real* you, not some fake hard rocker that you're pretending to be," Peter said.

"But I want to be *cool*," Matthew protested weakly.

"Cool like your friends want you to be, or cool because you stand for what's right?" Katie asked him quietly. Matthew looked from his sister to his brother, not knowing what to say.

"I've always admired you, bro, because you do what's right, no matter what," Peter said, meeting his brother's eyes. "That's why I call you 'My Number One Example.'"

At the moment, this didn't make Matthew feel any better. In fact, it made him feel worse.

"Thank you," he said to Peter, with a rueful smile. "Brad and Jason were just so excited about the whole thing. I guess I didn't really think about the example I would set."

Matthew tied the last bag of leaves and dragged it slowly to the curb—his shoulders slumped, and his face full of worry. And as he walked, he thought to himself, *I have really made a mess of things, haven't I?*

Chapter Two

Anything but Friendly

The front door creaked open and then slammed shut, announcing Grandma's arrival at the work party underway in her front yard. She watched Matthew walk slowly to the curb, dragging a big bag of leaves behind him. He deposited it on the curb and trudged up the driveway. His shoulders sagged, and he appeared to be deep in thought.

"What's the matter with Matthew?" asked Grandma, as she drew up alongside Peter, who was gathering up the yard tools.

"Oh, he just has a little problem, and he isn't sure how to fix it," Peter told Grandma over his shoulder, on his way to the garage to put the rakes away.

Grandma looked to Katie for an answer. "What kind of problem?" she asked.

"He just told us that he is running for student council," Katie began.

"That's great!" Grandma said.

"It would be, Grandma, but his friends want him to sing a hard rock song at the election assembly," Katie explained.

"We told him it wasn't the kind of song that someone who likes to do what's right would sing," Peter added, back from the garage.

"Now he doesn't know how to get out of singing it without disappointing his friends, and he's afraid he won't get elected without their support," Katie concluded.

"Oh, I see," Grandma said, nodding her head knowingly. "I think I have just the thing for him. Matthew," she called to her grandson, "are you ready to go to the art cottage? I've got a great new painting all ready to show you."

"I guess so," Matthew responded back, trying to sound excited.

"I get to go first this time," Peter cried. "Grandma, do you have the key?"

"It's right here," she said, and she pulled it out of her pocket, dangling it in midair. It glistened in the afternoon sun, sparkling with the promise of another incredible adventure. "But don't forget your journals!"

Peter bounded ahead, grabbed the backpack holding the children's journals, and planted himself outside the blue door to the little backyard house.

"Somehow," Katie mused, "Peter seems to get more than his share of going first." She and Grandma shared a laugh. Matthew shuffled behind them, still troubled by his dilemma.

"All right, kids, here we go," Grandma said when she reached the door. "Believe . . . ," she started, waiting for their response.

"In the wonder," Katie and Peter chimed in unison.

"Believe . . . ," Grandma said again.

"If you dare," Katie and Peter answered. Matthew stood silently by, looking at the ground.

"Believe in your heart . . . ," Grandma said as she took Matthew's chin in her hands and lifted it until he met her eyes, then waited expectantly for him to speak.

"Just believe and you're there," he finally mumbled reluctantly, managing a weak smile.

Grandma turned the key in the lock and opened the door to the wondrous world of her art cottage. As usual, the new painting was perched on the large easel in the middle of the room, draped with a white cloth. And as usual, the suspense was almost more than the children could bear.

Katie and Peter plopped themselves enthusiastically on the floor pillows at the foot of the easel and gazed upward at the shrouded painting. Matthew slowly lowered himself onto his pillow and rested his chin in his hands, looking distracted and miserable.

Grandma pretended not to notice and went on as if nothing was wrong. But all the while, she kept an eye on her unhappy grandson.

"Peter, would you like to do the unveiling honors today?" she invited.

"Of course I would!" He jumped up and stood at attention beside the painting, waiting for Grandma's go-ahead cue.

"All right, honey, we're ready," Grandma prompted him.

He flung the blanket off the painting and stood right in front of it, examining every inch of the colorful scene. "Hey, that's Daniel, isn't it?"

"Okay, buddy, time to sit down! We can't see a thing," Matthew begged Peter, yanking on his T-shirt. Grandma was glad to see that the promise of another story seemed to take Matthew's mind off his election predicament.

Peter quickly joined Matthew and Katie on the pillows, and together the three children studied Grandma's new painting.

The painting showed the inside of a deep, earthen pit. The top opened to the sky, but the opening was mostly covered by what looked like a huge, flat stone. At the stone's edge, in a spot where it didn't quite obscure the opening completely, small shafts of sunlight peeked through.

On the dirt floor of the pit, a man knelt in prayer. Resting on the ground just beside him were three docile lions, looking more like overgrown cats than ferocious beasts.

An angel, dressed in white, stood nearby in the

air, seemingly protecting the kneeling man. The angelic being glowed with such radiant light that his presence illuminated the dark cave.

"You are right, Peter. This man is Daniel," Grandma said, confirming his guess. "Now, I'll read the story, although you'll quickly discover that the story begins well before Daniel ends up in the lions' den. Just sit back and get comfortable, kids, and imagine that you're there."

Grandma picked up her worn Bible and began reading. "'It pleased [King] Darius to set over the kingdom an hundred and twenty princes, which should be over the whole kingdom.'"

Every time Grandma had painted a picture about a scripture story and then read the story to the children in the art cottage, the painting that depicted that story had come to life. And so, in eager anticipation, the children searched her new painting for even the slightest movement.

The more Grandma read, the more Matthew's interest seemed to grow, and so Grandma continued reading, rocking gently in her chair. "'And over these three presidents; of whom Daniel was the first . . . this Daniel was preferred above the

presidents and princes, because an excellent spirit was in him; and the king thought to set him over the whole realm.'"

"Ooh, look!" Katie whispered in alarm, pointing to the painting. "That lion is moving." Indeed, one of the lions stretched its front paws, rolled onto its side, and seemed to go to sleep. "Do we have to go *there*?"

"First of all," Matthew whispered back, "I have no intention of going *into* the lions' den. We'll just be going *near* it. Second, I don't think we'll arrive when Daniel is in the den. Grandma said that happened later in the story."

"I guess you're right," Katie muttered, but she didn't seem completely convinced. "But let's enter the picture *above* that pit, okay? I don't want to end up anywhere near those lions."

"Well, what are we waiting for?" Peter insisted quietly, so as not to alert Grandma. "Let's go!" And with an impish grin on his face, he offered one hand to his brother and the other to his sister.

Matthew grabbed his brother's hand with gusto. Katie closed her eyes, crossed her fingers, and gingerly reached out to Peter. Then Matthew rose up on his knees and, just as Katie had requested, pressed his free hand into the painting well above the den of lions.

WHOOSH! That was all it took, and the children were lifted up and away, beyond the walls of Grandma's art cottage. Strong winds whipped their hair, and powerful streams of air swirled around them from the tops of their heads to the tips of their toes. The trip was intense, but short.

Six feet touched the ground as the children were deposited atop a small hill, right near a large stone disk. They recognized it immediately as the stone that partially covered the pit filled with lions.

But before investigating further, Matthew had a good look at himself. Just as in each scripture adventure before, his T-shirt and jeans were replaced with other clothing. This time, he was wearing a heavy leather tunic that looked like a sleeveless shirt on top. But on the bottom—*oh no!* he thought silently—it looked decidedly like a *skirt*. Both boys—recognizing that their clothing would be considered girlish in the twenty-first century—made disgusted faces as they examined themselves. "Yu-u-u-cck!" Peter said, expressing what they both were feeling.

Hearing an angry roar, Peter ran to the pit's edge and peeked through the uncovered spot to get a good look at the deadly beasts. He leaned so far into the opening that half of his body disappeared.

Alarmed, Matthew and Katie ran to their brother, and each grabbed one of his legs to keep him from falling into the den.

"Let go of me," he protested. "I'm all right."

"That's not what it looked like to us," Katie told him.

"We're just trying to keep you safe, buddy," Matthew explained.

"On second thought," Peter said, looking again over the edge of the deep pit, "those lions don't seem so friendly, do they?"

A loud laugh from behind them startled the children. "Friendly? Those lions are *anything* but friendly!"

Chapter Three

Duty Calls

The children wheeled around to discover a boy about Matthew's age with an amused look on his face. "You don't have much experience with lions, do you?" He was carrying a large wooden bucket that he set down right near the rim of the pit that held the hungry lions.

"As a matter of fact, we have no experience with lions at all," Matthew told him.

"That is exactly what I thought," the boy said. "I have never seen you around here before. Are you new here?"

"Brand new. It's our first day," Peter explained.

"Have you been assigned your duties yet?" the boy asked.

"Duties?" Matthew sounded confused. "Uh . . .

19

no . . . , we don't have any duties yet," Matthew replied truthfully, straightening his leather tunic and trying to look calm. "Actually, we are just visiting here for a day or two. Then we must return home."

"I see," the boy said thoughtfully. "Well then, come, you can help me feed the lions. My name is Elam. I am a servant here in the palace of King Darius." Elam bowed slightly from the waist as he spoke.

"Glad to meet you, Elam. I am Matthew," Matthew said and returned the bow. "And this is my brother, Peter, and my sister, Katie."

Peter bowed low with a flourish, and Katie nodded her head demurely.

Elam smiled at her. "Katie? That is a name I haven't heard before. It is very unusual, but . . ." He thought for a moment. "I like it," he declared.

"Come." Elam motioned for them to follow him forward to the precipice of the pit. "Let us feed these lions."

He removed the heavy wooden lid from his bucket. It was filled with fresh lamb's meat for the lions. "Take some and throw it in the opening where the stone does not quite cover the den. That little opening lets the lions get fresh air to breathe, and it allows me to throw in food when they are hungry."

"Aren't they *always* hungry?" Katie asked with a grimace on her face, not sure she wanted to hear the answer.

"They get hungry when no one has been sent into the pit as punishment. When someone is sentenced to the lions' den, believe me, these beasts have plenty to eat." Elam picked up some fresh meat, held it over the small opening, and dropped it to the waiting lions.

Following suit, Matthew and Peter scooped up some meat and threw it into the deep den. Katie, horrified by the idea, stayed in the background, waiting for the feeding to be finished.

The boys, looking down into the den, watched as the lions devoured the meat, tearing it easily with their large teeth and chewing it effortlessly in their enormous jaws.

Peter's eyes got big as he watched. "I see what you mean, Elam. Those lions really *are* wild, aren't they?"

"Exactly," Elam agreed. "Now it is time for the king's noonday meal. You can help me prepare and serve it." He led them from the lions' enclosure along the open air corridors that rimmed the inner courtyard of the king's large, grand palace.

"This looks a little like the palace where Esther lived," Katie whispered to Matthew.

"That's because it *is* the palace where Esther lived, only we're here a lot earlier than when she lived here," Matthew informed her.

"Yeah, so this king will be a different king. I'll bet that's him on that carving right there," Peter surmised. Carved into the stone mural on the wall was a magnificent winged sphinx with the bearded head of the king on its shoulders. An ornate golden crown adorned the top of its head.

Legions of the king's army were depicted marching along the corridor walls. Elam pointed them out. "Those are the warriors of the army that destroyed Jerusalem, where my people lived, and brought them here as captives."

"You were taken *captive*?" Matthew asked.

"No, not me. It was my grandparents, along with all the Jews," Elam replied. "They were lucky to be assigned to work in the palace, where my family has worked ever since. I have a safe place to live, and food is plentiful."

They entered the massive, hectic kitchen where dozens of servants worked feverishly over open fire pits, preparing the king's noonday meal. Large pottery platters were laid out on long wooden counters, each waiting to be filled with food.

"Elam!" the head cook called out. "It is your job today to prepare the platters for Daniel, Shadrach, Meshach, and Abed-nego. Remember, no meat."

"Why no meat?" Peter asked Elam.

"When Jerusalem was conquered, the king ordered the young captive men of royal Jewish lineage to come here to the palace. He chose the smartest and most skilled boys to live here and be trained in the language and the traditions of the Chaldeans—which is the language and the traditions of the king and his royal palace. Daniel, Shadrach, Meshach, and Abed-nego were some of the Jewish boys specially chosen by the king," Elam began his explanation.

"What does that have to do with not eating meat?" Peter wanted to know.

"Patience, Peter," Elam said, "I'm getting to that. Part of the previous king's training program included providing meat and wine for the boys to partake of, and he expected obedience. But Jewish law sets forth strict rules for preparing and eating meat. So Daniel, Shadrach, Meshach, and Abednego asked to be served only vegetables, grains, seeds, and water for ten days. At the end of ten days, they looked so much better than those who filled up on meat and wine that they were allowed to eat as they wished forever after. Now, although they are older, they are still strong and healthy."

"They looked *that* much better after avoiding meat for just ten days?" Katie asked, amazed by such results.

"I think it was more than not eating meat. I think God blessed them because they were obedient to His laws. He also blessed them with knowledge and wisdom. Daniel was especially blessed to understand visions and dreams. This king has put great trust in Daniel's words, just as the two kings before him did."

"Elam! Are the platters ready?" the chief cook called impatiently.

"Almost," Elam answered. "Here's where I will need your help, my friends." Elam then instructed Katie, Matthew, and Peter: "Katie, will you fill these bowls with almonds and pistachio nuts, and put them in the middle of this platter? Then arrange the figs, pomegranates, and grapes around the bowls."

While Katie chose the best fruit to display on her platter, Elam gathered cucumbers, beans, and leeks for Matthew to arrange on another tray. He handed Peter a golden pitcher. "Peter, you fill this pitcher with water from that barrel," and he pointed to a large wooden cauldron in the corner of the kitchen.

"Right," Peter replied, taking his task very seriously. Using the wooden ladle hanging above the barrel, Peter dipped cool water into the ornate pitcher.

Elam took a large bowl from a shelf and filled it with a thick lentil stew that was bubbling over an open fire. He placed it in the center of another platter and surrounded it with thick wedges of

wheat bread and chunks of white cheese. He finished off the nutritious display with a handful of olives and a few mint leaves.

"That all looks wonderful," Elam said, examining each platter, "and so artistic!" He nodded special approval to Katie, as he looked over her handiwork. "Thanks to all your help, friends, we are ready to go. Katie, Matthew, and I will each take a platter. Peter, you carry the pitcher of water. Now, let us serve the meal without delay."

The children lined up behind Elam, and with great ceremony, they joined the procession parading into the king's grand dining hall. At its entrance, the king's servants paused to part billowy green curtains that hung from tall white marble pillars. And with the parting, the splendor of the sumptuous royal dining hall was revealed to the eyes of three awestruck children from the latter days.

Chapter Four

Jealous Hearts and an Excellent Spirit

As the curtains parted and they entered the royal dining hall, Katie, Matthew, and Peter took in the lavish décor all around them. Marble pillars lined the perimeter of the enormous room. Yards of shimmering blue and green curtains hung from silver rods spanning the space between each pillar and were elegantly tied back with heavy purple cords.

The servers marched with their laden platters to their appointed places surrounding the long center table. Then, as if on cue, each stepped back ceremoniously and stood silently at attention.

But the children followed Elam to a table set apart in one corner of the great hall. Copying

Elam precisely, they stood erect with their platters and pitcher.

"Good job," he whispered. "Now, we will wait until the king is served. Then we will serve Daniel, Meshach, Shadrach, and Abed-nego."

"Where are they?" Peter whispered back.

"Right in front of us," Elam replied, indicating four men who reclined on gold lounge chairs— almost like beds—placed alongside the table, so that the incline of their heads positioned their mouths near their plates.

"Why does everyone here lie down to eat?" Peter whispered to Katie.

"I don't know, but it looks kind of fun, if you ask me," she replied softly.

"I don't think Mom would go for it," Peter said with a smile.

"You're right about that," Matthew agreed wholeheartedly. "Seems like a good way to spill food all over. And you know how much Mom loves a mess!"

At the front of the hall, the king rested on a magnificent gold bed atop a raised platform.

Behind the bed, a line of servants gently waved fans to cool him.

With a quick, double clap of his hands, the chief steward signaled for the food to be brought forward. One by one, each server in turn mounted the platform and held his tray out for the king to examine. Then, after each presentation, the steward waited for the king's nod of approval, indicating that he'd like to eat what was displayed on the platter. When the nod was given, the steward grandly served food from the platter onto the king's plate. Once, when the king shook his head "no" in response to a platter, the servant holding it quickly stepped down, seeming almost embarrassed that the king had refused his offering.

When the king's plate was full and his wine goblet filled, the steward clapped his hands again. The rest of the servers stepped forward and the remainder of the food was distributed to the princes in the hall.

Elam offered his platter to Daniel first. As Daniel took several chunks of wholesome wheat bread, he greeted Elam affectionately. "Shalom, Elam." He whispered the Jewish greeting softly, so that the other princes, reclining near the main table, couldn't hear him.

"Shalom," Elam whispered, a faint smile on his lips.

"I have not seen these servants before," Daniel said, nodding toward Katie, Matthew, and Peter.

"No, they are visitors from afar. They are good friends of mine," Elam explained.

Daniel smiled. "Then they are my friends too."

Katie and Matthew served the four men from their platters, and Peter followed after them with the clean, cool water from his pitcher. When they had filled their plates, the four Jewish princes paused and offered a prayer of thanks to God.

As they enjoyed their simple, nourishing meal, Daniel, Shadrach, Meshach, and Abed-nego talked of the blessings they had received from God.

"I will never forget how we were delivered from the fiery furnace by the power of God," Meshach said.

"It was truly a miracle," Shadrach agreed, as he remembered the fear that had gripped him when he saw the blazing furnace. "But we were sent to the furnace because we were true to God," he went on, remembering how they had refused to worship the golden image set forth by an earlier king, "so God blessed us."

"He certainly did. Surely, God sent the angel that protected us from the flame," Abed-nego remembered. "Not a hair on our head was singed, nor was even the smell of fire upon us. And in the end, our terrible fear was turned to peace."

"How great is our God," Daniel proclaimed. "There is, indeed, protection and joy when we live as God has commanded."

As they talked, Matthew noticed several men across the hall who looked at the four Jewish princes with disdain. Their dislike for Daniel and his friends was unmistakable.

"What is the matter with them?" Matthew asked Elam, nodding to the unhappy princes.

"They are advisors and princes to the king. They dislike Daniel and all Jews," he replied.

"What has Daniel done wrong?" Katie asked.

"He hasn't done anything wrong. The other princes are jealous because Daniel is trusted so much by the king," Elam explained quietly.

At that moment, a trumpet sounded through

the hall, and the room fell silent. The king's chamberlain stood and cried, "The king will now make a declaration."

The king sipped a last drink of wine from his goblet. Then he took his sceptre in hand and stood to address the princes. "It pleases me to set over the kingdom an hundred and twenty princes," he began. "Over these I will set three presidents, unto whom the princes shall be accountable." All eyes were on the king, who paced the length of the platform as he spoke, his royal robes flowing behind him.

The princes all listened attentively to every word King Darius spoke. The prideful anticipation in their faces revealed the unmistakable hope of each prince that he, himself, would be chosen as one of the three presidents.

But, instead of revealing who the three powerful presidents would be, the king announced who would rule over them. "It pleases me to declare before you that I have chosen to set Daniel above these three presidents. In addition, I have decided to set him over the whole realm," the king declared boldly. "He shall govern my kingdom."

A dark cloud of jealousy passed over the faces of the men at the center table. They could barely hide the outrage they felt inside. None of them could bring himself to look at the king or at Daniel.

The king continued his address. "Daniel has been blessed by God with many gifts. And I have come to trust his counsel and his advice. He is filled with wisdom and knowledge, and most important, he has an excellent spirit in him. For these reasons, I commend him to you with all my heart."

The king acknowledged Daniel with his raised sceptre, and his chamberlain raised his goblet high in a toast to Daniel.

Shadrach, Meshach, and Abed-nego raised their goblets with the king's chamberlain, but theirs contained water, not wine. With the chamberlain, they heartily drank to Daniel.

And although the unsmiling princes in the center of the room raised their goblets too, observant Matthew noticed that they pridefully refused to drink.

Chapter Five

Sinister, but Brilliant

Matthew tapped Elam on the shoulder, "Did you see that?" he asked.

"Yes, I saw," he replied, watching as about a dozen of the princes huddled together conspiratorially around the center table in the middle of the dining hall.

"I wonder what they are saying," Matthew said.

"One can only guess," Elam replied. "But it looks as if my fellow servants could use some help serving the last of the meal over there. Why don't we go help, and perhaps we can hear what they are saying?"

"I've always wanted to be a spy," Peter said

as his eyes sparkled at the chance to test out his techniques.

"Now you can stop practicing on me," Matthew told his younger brother, as he rolled his eyes and prepared to follow Elam.

"I think I will stay here," Katie said, deciding that she felt safe right where she was. "I don't like the look of those men. I'll see that Daniel and his friends have everything they need."

"Good idea, Sis. You can see us from here. We'll be right back," Matthew assured her.

Katie picked up her tray of fruit and offered it once again to Daniel, Meshach, Shadrach, and Abed-nego, who smiled gratefully and politely thanked her.

"All right, boys," Elam instructed Matthew and Peter. "Follow me, and do what I do."

"Roger!" Peter saluted.

"Roger? What does that mean? I have never heard that word before."

Matthew elbowed Peter and whispered, "They don't use that phrase here. You are going to give us away if you aren't more careful."

"Oh, yeah, I forgot," Peter mumbled. And

then to Elam, "'Roger' is just my funny way of saying 'Yes, sir.'"

Elam laughed, "Oh, I see. Well, then let us go!"

Elam gave them each a tray. "Follow me to the center table. And," he teased, "try to look like you know what you are doing."

Peter and Matthew lifted trays onto their shoulders and followed Elam along the perimeter of the dining hall.

"Stop! Where do you think you are going?" It was one of the king's stewards who stood, blocking their way.

Matthew's heart was beating wildly. He just hoped he wouldn't spill his tray and that he wouldn't have to speak.

Peter, on the other hand, stood beside Matthew with a big smile on his face, pretending not to be scared. *That's how real spies do it*, he told himself.

Elam met the steward's suspicious gaze. "Sir, we noticed that some trays on the center table were empty. Ours are still quite full. So we are going to offer them to the princes over here."

The steward softened a little. "Very well, you

may pass." He stood aside, but he kept his eyes on the boys until they reached the princes' table.

The princes lay on their lounging couches, talking among themselves. They didn't notice the three boy-servants approach with more food. Apparently, the princes thought themselves too important to take notice of servants, so they talked freely of their feelings about the king's announcement and Daniel.

"How is it that the king exalts Daniel, the Jew?" one of the princes, a man named Kish, asked angrily.

"It makes no sense to me either, Kish. The ruler over all the princes should be one of us, not a Jew," another young prince, named Jeshem, answered him.

"I have never liked Daniel. The king thinks he is so wise. But I don't think he is any wiser than *I* am. Why didn't the king promote me or even you, Jeshem?" Kish sounded frustrated and deflated.

"You are the wise one, Kish. You should have been named. But there is nothing we can do about it now. The king has made the decree, and it cannot be reversed."

Elam came forward with his tray of food and offered it to Jeshem. The haughty prince looked disdainfully at Elam as he heaped a large helping of food onto his plate.

"Boy, come here," Kish demanded, turning abruptly to Peter. Peter, unaware that Kish's order was directed at him, stood at attention without moving, obviously taking his job very seriously. "You," Kish glared and pointed directly at Peter, "I said come here, boy."

Peter stepped forward quickly and blurted, "Yes, sir. What do you wish, sir?"

"I wish to have some of the fruit on your tray! What else do you think I would want with a mere servant?" Kish was snarling now, as he scooped up handfuls of fruit from Peter's tray.

"There must be a way to rid ourselves of Daniel," Jeshem said, as he rested his head against his lounge pillow. He closed his eyes, deep in thought. After a long pause, a menacing sneer crept slowly across his face. He opened his eyes, a plot clearly taking shape in his mind. He started to laugh—a cruel, mocking laugh.

"What is it? What has your mean little mind come up with now?" Kish asked, a glimmer of sinister hope sparkling in his beady eyes.

"Have you noticed how pious Daniel is?" Jeshem asked Kish. "It is very inspiring, isn't it?" His words were civil, but his voice was cold and hard.

"I suppose you are referring to the prayers he offers three times a day to his Jewish god," Kish said, catching on.

"Exactly. Three times a day he faces toward Jerusalem. I mean, he faces toward what *was* Jerusalem. After the conquest, it now lies in ruins, with the Jews' precious temple knocked down, right to the ground!" Jeshem sneered and chortled as he spoke.

The hair on the back of Matthew's neck stood up as he listened to Jeshem and Kish. He did not like the tone of their voices at all. He looked sideways at Elam and Peter, who, from the looks on their faces, didn't like the princes' talk any better than he did.

"Well, I have an idea. A very good idea," Jeshem continued, his eyes narrowing. "Would you like to hear it?"

"Go on, Jeshem," Kish said, his anticipation growing. "I am listening."

"It is simple, really. Let us go to the king and propose that whosoever should ask anything of anyone besides the king shall be cast into the den of lions." Jeshem continued, laying out his plan, "We will tell him that petitioning someone other than King Darius is a way of showing loyalty and gratitude to someone else. And the loyalty of Daniel—he who will govern the king's whole realm—should be given to the king alone, and to none other."

"It is brilliant, simply brilliant," Kish said gleefully.

Peter sucked in his breath, and his eyes got wide with worry. He looked helplessly to Matthew and Elam in shocked silence. All three boys couldn't help remembering the strength of the lions' powerful jaws and the sharpness of their teeth.

"Jeshem, we cannot go to the king alone. We must persuade others to support us in this plan to expose disloyalty to the throne," Kish said.

"Oh, that will not be hard." Jeshem sounded very sure of himself. "You and I know many princes who will stand behind us. Now is the time for us to unite, if we want to rid ourselves of Daniel for good. Come, let us gather support for our plan."

They got up from their beds and pushed rudely past Matthew, Peter, and Elam, nearly knocking their trays to the floor. From the other side of the room, Katie looked on, unmistakable dread filling her heart.

Chapter Six

To Him I Will Be True

"Daniel is in real trouble." Elam sounded despondent, and he eyed the princes suspiciously as they embarked on their devious campaign against Daniel.

"What do you think they are saying now?" Matthew asked Elam, his voice full of concern.

"I think we are going to know shortly," Elam answered, pointing to Peter, who had positioned himself between Jeshem and an unknown prince, a tray of fruit in his hands. Peter winked at Elam and innocently proffered more fruit to the two men.

Jeshem took the offered fruit. "Surely you agree that the king is the foremost authority in the land," he began, preparing to turn this prince, too, against Daniel.

"Certainly. Who else would it be?" the prince responded.

"Well, I would say that Daniel is coming awfully close," Jeshem said.

At the mention of Daniel's name, the unknown prince frowned and lowered his voice. "Unfortunately, that is true. Why do we have to be subject to a Jew?"

"My question exactly," Jeshem agreed. "I will never understand why the king has chosen *him* as the favored one, above any of us." Then Jeshem lowered his voice even further, as if he were about to tell a valuable secret. "But I believe there is a solution to our problem."

The other prince, not wanting to be left out of any plot, encouraged Jeshem to go on. "I've seen that look in your eye before," he flattered Jeshem. "You are really onto something, aren't you? You can tell me, Jeshem. I have always been loyal to you."

"Yes, I suppose I can trust you." Jeshem paused dramatically. Then he spoke slowly, as if he were revealing the location of hidden treasure. "Suppose there were a way to rid ourselves of Daniel, and at the same time turn the king's favor toward us?"

Peter's grip on his tray loosened, and the remaining fruit tumbled onto the floor.

Startled by figs rolling over his bare toes, Jeshem wheeled around to discover Peter standing right behind him. He grabbed Peter by the arm and demanded, "Why are you still here? Have you heard our conversation?"

"Me?" Peter smiled innocently, but his heart was thumping loudly in his chest. "I only wanted to know if you were finished with the fruit."

"No, we don't want any more fruit, you fool!" Jeshem shoved Peter to the ground.

"Calm yourself, Jeshem," the other prince warned. "We do not want to be noticed."

"Pick up that fruit and get out of here," Jeshem hissed at Peter through clenched teeth.

Peter quickly retrieved the fruit and made a beeline for Elam and Matthew.

The children, now too far away to hear the low voices of the conniving princes, watched as Jeshem

apparently laid out his plan to the prince, his arms waving wildly about, and his eyes full of cunning.

Elam and the children quickly gathered the empty food platters and hurried to the kitchen to begin the preparations for dinner.

"You should have seen the look in Jeshem's eyes when he realized you were still standing there, Peter. I thought you were done for," Matthew admitted, as he helped Katie wash the mountains of plates and goblets used at the midday meal. He threw Peter a soft piece of material. "Here, we need some help drying these dishes."

"Hasn't anyone here heard of paper plates?" Peter wondered out loud.

"What do you mean *paper* plates? Do you mean plates made from writing parchment?" Elam was puzzled. "How absurd! Parchment would tear under the weight of food. Or worse, disintegrate. And then it would be useless for writing. What a terrible waste!"

"Yes, Peter. Elam is right. The idea is preposterous!" Matthew shot a piercing look at Peter.

"Let us clean these dishes quickly," Elam

encouraged. "Then I will take you to the king's garden. I must gather vegetables and fruit for the king's evening meal." They worked as fast as they could.

Finally, when the last dish was dry and stacked on the crude wooden shelf where dishes were stored, they escaped into the garden. There, under the shelter of a fig tree, the children lay on their backs, looking up at the blue sky beyond the green umbrella of fig leaves floating over them.

Katie noticed that Elam was quiet and thoughtful. "Elam, what are you thinking about?" Katie asked kindly.

"My mother," he responded, with longing in his voice. "She died of the fever just last year."

"What about your father?" Katie asked him.

"He died when I was just a baby. And I was the firstborn, so I have no siblings. But I never feel alone, because God is always in my heart," Elam explained matter-of-factly.

Katie sighed. "That is wonderful, Elam."

"What do you remember about your mother?" Peter asked.

"I remember many things about her. Sometimes I forget exactly what she looked like, but I will never forget how I felt when she would hold me close and tell me about God." Somehow, Elam sounded sorrowful *and* peaceful at the same time. "The power of my mother's testimony is always with me."

"I wish we all could have known her." Katie smiled at him.

"She would have liked all of you," Elam said. "Wait! I think there *is* a way you could know her—at least a little."

"How?" Peter was curious.

"I will sing a song for you about God and His goodness. Mother made it up to sing to me when I was a little boy. I hope when I sing it, you can feel her faith in God and the power of her testimony, just like I do."

"We would love that," Katie said with conviction. And she and her brothers rolled over and rested their chins in their hands, as Elam's youthful voice rang out, filling both the king's garden and the children's hearts with gladness:

> *For home, for food, for family,*
> *For joy, for peace, for love,*

For all good things on earth, I give
My thanks to God above.

I'll bow to Him, I'll pray to Him,
I'll serve Him gladly, too.
He is my loving friend and Lord,
To Him I will be true.

Although sometimes our trials are great,
And we with sadness yearn,
Our God will turn our grief to joy
If to Him we will turn.

I'll bow to Him, I'll pray to Him,
I'll serve Him gladly, too.
He is my loving friend and Lord,
To Him I will be true.

Chapter Seven

More Precious Than Gold

Back in the cavernous kitchen, Elam and the children unloaded baskets of grapes, figs, pomegranates, beans, cucumbers, and leeks on the head cook's table. After singing to them in the garden, Elam had taught Katie, Matthew, and Peter how to choose the ripest fruits and vegetables from the king's abundant garden.

Now the head cook looked over their bounteous harvest and declared, "We will have a feast tonight, thanks to you, Elam. But there is no time to spare. Let us all work quickly. Elam, you take these three new servants"—he pointed to Matthew, Katie, and Peter—"and prepare the tables in the king's dining hall for the evening meal."

On their way to the dining hall, the children

caught sight of Jeshem and his friend, Kish, striding down the hall toward the king's private quarters.

"Look!" Peter said softly, backing into the shadows. "There they go to talk to the king."

Sure enough, Jeshem and Kish stopped at the door to the king's quarters. Jeshem spoke to the guard posted there. The guard knocked three times and stepped in to announce the arrival of the two princes. Meanwhile, Jeshem puffed out his chest, looking smug and full of himself. When the guard motioned for the princes to enter, Jeshem swept importantly past him, with Kish following close behind.

"That doesn't look good, does it?" Katie said uneasily.

"No, it does not," Elam replied. "Jeshem is out to get Daniel, and he will try every trick to do it."

"Maybe the king will put Jeshem in his place," Matthew said.

"That is my hope too. But the king is easily flattered." Elam sounded worried. "With God on his side, however, surely Daniel will prevail." He said this with more confidence than he felt.

Then Elam stepped out of the shadows and

led the way to the dining hall. There the children worked quickly to prepare for the evening meal.

Katie gasped as she pulled back a curtain concealing storage shelves for dishes. The wooden shelves were lined with goblets made entirely of polished gold. "I have never seen so much gold in all my life," she said breathlessly.

"Where did all this stuff come from?" Peter asked, his eyes wide with wonder.

"These," Elam said sadly, holding one of the exquisite goblets in his hand, "were stolen from the palace in Jerusalem when the city was conquered, and they were presented to King Nebuchadnezzar as some of the spoils of the conquest."

"But they didn't belong to him," Katie protested.

Elam laughed bitterly. "Have you ever heard the phrase 'to the victor go the spoils'?"

A quizzical look came over Peter's face.

"That means that whoever wins a war gets to take anything he wants from the loser. So when Jerusalem fell to Babylon, the Babylonian army claimed all Jerusalem's valuable treasures for its king," Elam explained.

"I'm sorry," Matthew said sympathetically. "It must be hard for you to see reminders of your family's homeland."

"Yes, it is hard. But it also reminds me that there are things more important than earthly treasures. No one can take my belief in God from me, and that is a treasure more precious than all this gold." Elam's eyes shone with faith and assurance as he spoke.

"Yes, you are right about that," said Matthew thoughtfully. Elam's simple testimony penetrated his heart, and for a moment, he thought about his own election predicament at school.

"Well, there is no time to dwell on that thought, friends," Elam reminded them. "We must finish preparing for the dinner."

"Yes, sir!" Peter said, remembering this time not to say 'Roger!' He gave Elam his best military salute, grabbed some goblets, and placed them carefully on the low tables between the reclining beds.

They worked until the table looked ready for dinner to be served and then returned to the kitchen to help with last-minute preparations.

Just as the last tray was filled, the king's chief steward entered the kitchen and clapped two times.

"The king and his party are ready for dinner," he announced loudly, and with great authority.

Along with the other servants, Elam, Matthew, Katie, and Peter hoisted heavily laden trays onto their shoulders and joined the procession to the dining hall. Once inside, they again positioned themselves near Daniel and his friends. Peter, for one, had had enough of Jeshem and his fellow conspirators, who sat smugly in the center of the room.

"Jeshem looks too happy," Peter observed.

"Yes, I'm a little worried," Katie said.

Daniel sat contentedly with his friends, eating fruits and vegetables, unaware of the vile plot now in motion.

As soon as the meal was served, a trumpet sounded, and a hush fell upon the room. Just as at the noonday meal, the king's chamberlain stood to address the princes.

"At the king's command, I will now read a decree, which is to be observed by every subject of the king." With great ceremony, he unrolled the scroll he held in his hands and began reading:

Because of the greatness of King Darius,
and in order to properly pay tribute
to his sovereign authority,
the throne makes the following decree:
"By royal declaration,
let it be known that for the next thirty days,
no man shall pray to any god
or ask anything of any man,
except it be King Darius.
If any man is found praying to any god
or asking anything of any man
he shall be cast into the den of lions."

Daniel and his friends sat with their heads bowed, struck to the core by the king's decree.

Jeshem, at the center table, held his head high and triumphant, reveling in his victory. He raised his goblet with a shout, toasting King Darius. The other princes followed his lead.

The king, seemingly unaware of the effect the law would have on Daniel, nodded his head in smiling approval, pleased at the attention that was lavished upon him by his princes.

"What shall we do?" one of Daniel's friends

asked in a tremulous voice. It was clear that Daniel, Shadrach, Meshach, and Abed-nego were shaken by this turn of events.

But Daniel's fear quickly turned to resolve, and he spoke with conviction. "I shall do what I have always done, my dear friends. I shall serve the true and living God. No matter the consequence, I will be true to Him."

From a middle section the children heard one prince say to another, after seeing Daniel's solemn reaction to the decree, "I thought Daniel was the king's favorite. How could the king do this to one he favors?"

Another prince replied, "The king has allowed himself to be swayed by cunning men. They have flattered him, and he is pleased with this law that sets him above all the gods."

"Don't they know there is only one God?" Peter whispered to Elam.

"Unfortunately, the Babylonians worship many gods and idols," Elam replied.

"I guess they haven't heard of the Ten Commandments, then," Peter said, puzzled by the whole thing. "It says right there, 'Thou shalt have no other gods before me.'"

"Well," Elam explained, "the Ten Commandments were given to the children of Israel, through the prophet, Moses. The Babylonians don't even believe that Moses was a prophet."

Matthew stood silently, listening to Peter and Elam. Katie noticed that he seemed extra pensive and serious—even for Matthew. "A penny for your thoughts," she prodded gently.

"A scripture has been running through my head," he replied. "It's a scripture from the Old Testament that I learned in Primary."

"Which one?" Katie asked.

"One that applies to me," he replied, as a resolute smile crept across his face. "It goes like this: 'Choose you this day whom ye will serve, . . . but as for me and my house, we will serve the Lord.'"

And then Matthew stood a little taller and spoke these words with confidence and clarity: "I have been thinking about the election. Katie, I think that today is the day that I must choose. And I am going to choose to serve the Lord, just like Daniel."

Chapter Eight

But If Not

It was not until the last goblet was returned to its shelf that the four weary children retired to the stables to sleep in the straw beside Elam.

"Before we go to sleep, would you kneel with me to pray?" Elam asked.

"Wh—wh—what if one of the king's men sees you and tells the king?" Katie's question held a hint of terror.

"Don't worry, friends. I am only a kitchen servant. No one will be watching to see if *I* am praying," Elam said, trying to quiet Katie's fears. "This trap was set for Daniel. He's the one who will be risking his life by praying to God."

"Then please go ahead, Elam," a calmer Katie

encouraged. "We are all in need of your prayers tonight."

The four children knelt in a dark corner of the stable with heads bowed, while Elam offered an earnest prayer.

Matthew found himself touched by the humble, heartfelt way that Elam spoke with God. *This boy truly knows Heavenly Father, almost like a friend,* Matthew thought. *No wonder he never feels alone, even without his mother and father here on earth.* And Matthew resolved in his heart to draw closer to God by praying more sincerely, like Elam.

"Amen," Elam closed the prayer.

"Amen," the children repeated after him. And they meant it.

In the silence that followed, Elam again sang the song his mother used to sing to him. The beautiful, soothing melody was the last thing the children heard before they fell fast asleep on the soft straw.

Matthew wasn't sure how long he had been asleep when he was jolted awake by a noisy contingent of men marching through the stable yard. He hurried to the stable door and, in the faint light cast by the single torch carried at the head of the procession, he witnessed many armed guards hurrying by, with Daniel bound as a captive in their midst.

He shook Elam by the shoulders and urged, "Wake up, wake up! I think they are taking Daniel to the lions' den."

Jeshem and Kish, looking smug and triumphant, led the procession. They were followed by Daniel and the armed guards, who treated their prisoner roughly and with disdain. They shoved Daniel rudely past the stable door and along the path that led to the pit filled with hungry lions. Without complaint, Daniel suffered the guards' abuse and ceaseless taunting.

A group of Jewish believers followed closely behind the procession. Elam recognized one of his friends among them. "Sherem," he called, "what is happening?"

Sherem rushed over to Elam. "Jeshem and Kish laid a trap for Daniel. They knew he would pray to our God, even though the king had forbidden it. So when Daniel knelt at his window for evening prayer, they were watching. As soon as they had their proof, they hurried to inform the king."

Suddenly, the glow of many blazing torches filled the stable yard. Alarmed, the children melted into the safety of the shadows. Six of the king's servants appeared, torches aloft, lighting the way for the king and his chamberlain.

The children could hear the two men talking as they passed. "You know you cannot change the decree, Your Majesty," the chamberlain was saying to a distraught King Darius. "The law does not permit it."

"I am the king. Do you not think I know the laws of my own kingdom?" the king lamented. "I was tricked into issuing that decree. I now see that it was a plot by jealous men to get rid of Daniel, my most trusted advisor."

"Sire, perhaps we should not go to the lions' den tonight," the chamberlain gently suggested, hoping to spare the king more despair.

"But I must speak to Daniel before . . . ," the king's voice trailed off.

Peter whispered, "I didn't know kings cried, but Darius is practically weeping!"

"I have never seen him so upset," Elam agreed. "Come, let us follow them."

"I'm not so sure that is a good idea," Katie protested.

"We'll stay safely in the shadows," Matthew told her. "We won't let ourselves be seen, I promise." With Matthew's assurance, Katie reluctantly went along.

Elam and the children silently followed the king and his servants, grateful for the glow from their torches that spilled onto the path, lighting the way in the dark night.

Very soon, the procession reached the small hill into which the deep pit for lions was carved. Daniel stood calmly in the torchlight as the king's guard removed the large stone disk covering the lions' den. Now the vicious snarling of the angry beasts could be clearly heard.

"Daniel, Daniel," the king cried when he saw

Daniel, waiting to be lowered into the deadly pit. "I have been deceived by cunning men!"

Jeshem and Kish, seeing the displeasure of the king, slunk into the black night, and disappeared before they were discovered.

"Forgive me, forgive me," the king begged Daniel. "I can do nothing. I am bound by the law. But the God whom you serve, He will deliver you." The king and Daniel embraced and then Daniel walked fearlessly, filled with faith, to the precipice of the pit. There, he grabbed hold of the rope the guards offered him, and they slowly lowered him into the cavernous den of lions.

The guards pushed and shoved the large stone back over the mouth of the den, until it was completely covered. Then the king sadly sealed the action by stamping a mark upon the stone with his signet ring, so that no one would remove it and free Daniel from the den.

In sorrow, the king turned away from the den and retraced his steps back to the palace. As he left, they heard him tell the chamberlain that he would return to the lions' den at the first rays of the morning sun to discover the fate of Daniel.

"We should return to the stable," Elam said. "It is not safe for us to be out here at night."

Back in the stable, the children lay awake, worried and unable to sleep. "Is it really possible that Daniel could be found alive and well in the morning?" Matthew wondered out loud.

"It would take a miracle," Peter said. "A big one."

"Shadrach, Meshach, and Abed-nego walked out of the fiery furnace unharmed. That was a miracle," Elam reminded them, "and a big one, at that."

"Why did that king put them in the fiery furnace in the first place?" Peter asked.

"Because they would not obey his decree to worship his golden image," Elam said. "When they were brought before the king to explain themselves, they boldly declared, 'If it be so, our God whom we serve is able to deliver us from the burning fiery furnace, and he will deliver us out of thine hand, O king. *But if not,* be it known unto thee, O king, that we will not serve thy gods, nor worship the golden image which thou hast set up.'"

"I bet that made the king mad," Peter said.

"It certainly did. In fact, he commanded that the furnace be heated hotter than it ever had been before. And they *still* came out alive."

"Well, that *was* a miracle," Peter agreed.

"So, let us pray for a miracle, and leave Daniel's fate in the Lord's hands," Elam suggested. "He seemed so full of faith, he probably feels like Shadrach, Meshach, and Abed-nego did. I can imagine him saying, just as they said, 'If it be so, my God whom I serve is able to deliver me from the lions' den. *But if not*, I will still pray to Him.'"

"'But if not.' Those are three important words, aren't they?" Matthew observed. And he thought again of the upcoming school election. He wondered if he would have the courage to say, "I know God could help me win this election, even without putting on a grungy, wild act. *But if not*, I will still be true to Him and behave like the believing person that I am."

And in the silence of the night, Matthew prayed that, even in the face of tremendous pressure from his friends, he would have the courage to be as true to God as Daniel was.

Chapter Nine

Because You Believe in Your God

Early in the morning, the sun's rays pierced the cracks in the rough wood slats of the stable walls. Still asleep in soft hay, Matthew's eyelids flickered as the sunlight danced on his face. The horses nearby pawed softly at the loamy soil in their stalls. A family of red finches, which claimed the stable's rafters as its home, chirped softly, signaling the start of a new day.

Matthew was not yet fully awake when the king's guard burst into the stable's outer yard, sending the chickens scurrying and clucking their noisy disapproval as they scattered. Matthew ran to the stable door and pressed one eye to a knothole, trying to see what was going on. He watched as the king, still dressed in the same clothes he wore the night before, pushed past his guards and disappeared down the path toward the lions' den.

"Come on," Matthew said, shaking the others awake. "The king is on his way to the lions' den."

"Right now? It's the middle of the night!" Peter complained groggily.

"It's morning, sleepyhead! Come on, let's go," Matthew prodded him.

"Oh, I hope he finds Daniel alive," Katie worried out loud.

"O, ye of little faith," Matthew chided her. "Don't forget, we know from the scriptures how this story ends."

"I have faith, but those lions! I never realized just how enormous and angry they were!" She shuddered as she thought about it.

Elam swung the stable door open, allowing the sunlight to rush in. "Come, friends, or we will not be there when the king removes his seal." Elam kicked Peter's foot. "I can get there before you."

"Oh no you can't!" Peter responded to the challenge by jumping up and darting out the door before Elam even realized what was happening.

Matthew grabbed Katie's hand, and together they ran to catch up to Peter and Elam.

When they neared the large stone disk over the lions' den, they took cover behind an outcropping of rock, peeking around it to see the events now unfolding.

"Break the seal," the king commanded, his voice filled with anxiety and fear. Sensing the urgency in the king's voice, the guards quickly pried up the seal atop the stone and, with great effort, removed the heavy stone from the mouth of the pit.

The king ran to the edge of the deep pit and peered in. But it was very dark, and he could not see Daniel. In desperation, he cried, "O Daniel, servant of the living God, is thy God, whom thou servest continually, able to deliver thee from the lions?"

His heart pounded as he waited for an answer, but none came. "Daniel!" he cried again, despairing.

Out of the darkness of the pit, Daniel stepped slowly into the shaft of light that shone from

above. In a strong, sure voice, he called to the king. "O king, live forever."

He was alive! In gratitude, the king sank to his knees, and buried his head in his hands. "I have passed the night fasting," he began to explain, relief filling his heavy heart. "Sleep would not come, neither could music console me. I was tormented by the thought of you in this pit with the lions."

Daniel raised his hand toward heaven, and testified to the king, "My God hath sent his angel, and hath shut the lions' mouths, that they have not hurt me." Then, humbly, and with deep sincerity, he declared, "Before thee, O king, have I done no hurt."

The king knew the words Daniel spoke were true. He had allowed himself to be tricked by jealous and cunning men. But now he could see things clearly, and his only concern was to free Daniel and restore him to his rightful position in the kingdom.

"Guards! Guards! Bring him up out of the den," the king commanded forcefully.

The guards rushed to the mouth of the pit and

threw a rope over the edge. Daniel grabbed hold, and they slowly pulled him up, until he clambered into the morning sunlight.

The king clasped Daniel by the arm and pulled him close in a warm embrace. "I can see no manner of hurt upon you," the king observed, after examining Daniel thoroughly. "And this because you believe in your God," he marveled.

"I think I feel as relieved as the king does," Katie breathed in a whisper.

Matthew put a reassuring hand on her shoulder. "I know how you feel, Sis. We are all very relieved."

"Our God *is* a God of miracles," Elam said, his voice filled with both conviction and wonder.

The king took Daniel by the arm, and together they started along the path back to the palace.

"Come," Elam said softly, "we don't want to be discovered. Let us go quickly to the kitchen and prepare some food for Daniel and the king."

"That's a good idea," Peter agreed readily. "I know that *I'm* always *starving* after I fast."

They raced ahead and reached the empty kitchen, panting and out of breath. Now familiar with the place, Katie grabbed a tray and set it on the counter. Matthew placed figs and grapes around its perimeter, and Elam tore chunks of brown bread, piling them in the center.

"This will ease their hunger," Elam said, looking over the nutritious spread. "I will take this to the king's table, so it is waiting when Daniel and the king arrive." He hoisted the tray onto his shoulder, and, with a smile, walked through the door, leaving the latter-day children alone in the kitchen.

Matthew watched him leave, and a wave of sadness suddenly swept over him. Katie could almost read his thoughts. She put her hand gently on his arm.

"I think it's time," she said softly.

"I know," he replied. "I feel it, too."

Even Peter knew the time had come to return to the art cottage. Without a word of protest (which was highly unusual for him), he offered one hand to Katie and the other to Matthew. After one last look around the kitchen, they grabbed hold. Immediately, the air swirled around them, lifting them off the earthen floor.

Katie, Matthew, and Peter didn't open their eyes until they felt the soft pillows cushion their arrival in the art cottage. They let out a collective sigh as they settled in and listened as Grandma finished reading the king's decree in the final verses of the chapter:

"'I make a decree, that in every dominion of my kingdom men tremble and fear before the God of Daniel: for he is the living God, and steadfast forever. . . . He delivereth and rescueth, and he worketh signs and wonders in heaven and in earth, who hath delivered Daniel from the power of the lions.'"

Grandma concluded, "So this Daniel prospered in the reign of Darius."

And then she closed her Bible.

Chapter Ten

I Will Serve the Lord

"Well, what did you think about that?" Grandma asked her three grandchildren as she removed her reading glasses.

"Wait, Grandma," Peter interrupted. "I missed the part about what happened to Jeshem and Kish."

"Who? What are you talking about?" Grandma asked, looking completely perplexed. "Jeshem? Kiss?"

"You know, Grandma—the men who tricked the king into making the decree that got Daniel into trouble," Peter said, sounding very sure of himself.

"There you go again," Matthew teased, winking at his brother. "What an imagination you have—making up names for characters in the story!"

"My, my, my," Grandma laughed. "You can really make a story come alive, Peter dear."

"So can you, Grandma," Peter said. "*Really* alive."

"Anyway," Katie interjected, steering the conversation in a different direction, "what *did* happen to those men? I guess we were distracted during that part."

"The king ordered *them* to face the same punishment as Daniel had to face. They were thrown into the lions' den." Grandma reviewed the story. "But I don't imagine they had the same heavenly protection."

"Ewwww, let's not think about it anymore," Katie begged.

"Good idea," Grandma agreed. "I'm anxious to hear what you thought about the story. Matthew, you usually have good insights. Any thoughts?"

Matthew smiled and said gratefully, "Grandma, you must have been inspired to paint this picture especially for me."

"Really? How is that?" she asked knowingly.

"Well, you know how I'm running for student council," he began, and then paused. Grandma nodded for him to go on.

"And I really want to win . . ."

"Duh!" Peter couldn't help interrupting. "Why else would you run for office?"

"Would you please let me finish?" Matthew said, glaring at Peter.

Peter rolled his eyes, locked his lips with an imaginary key, threw it over his shoulder, and waited silently for Matthew to continue.

"I have some friends . . ."

"So-called 'friends,'" Peter blurted out and then clamped his hand over his mouth. "Sorry," he said between his fingers, "it won't happen again. I promise."

Matthew ignored this last outburst and continued with his story. "Instead of me giving a speech, these friends want me to sing a song with my guitar."

"That seems like a clever idea. I love to hear you play your guitar," Grandma said encouragingly.

"The problem is, they want me to sing new words to a song by the Grunge Worms."

"Worms that sing?" Obviously, Grandma had never heard of the Grunge Worms.

"No, that's the name of a hard rock band. Anyway, just for fun, they want me to dress in a black motorcycle jacket and spike my hair up and use a really loud electric guitar."

"Somehow that doesn't sound like you. Is that what you want people to think you're really like?" Grandma asked kindly.

Matthew stared at the painting of Daniel humbly kneeling in front of the ferocious lions. "No," he finally answered quietly. "I want to win, and these friends convinced me that this was the only way to do it," and then he hung his head and said quietly, "so I agreed."

And then Matthew drew in a deep breath, raised his head, squared his shoulders, and spoke with deep meaning. "But, when I look at Daniel, so firm in his decision to worship God no matter the cost, I see things very differently."

"How so?" Grandma coaxed.

"I believe in God. So everything I do and say should be an example to my friends of what He teaches," Matthew said thoughtfully. "I've been thinking about a scripture from the Old Testament. It goes like this: 'Choose you this day whom ye will serve, . . . but as for me and my house, we will serve the Lord.' I think it's time for me to choose." Matthew sighed a heavy sigh. "I guess I'll just have to think of another way to convince everyone to vote for me."

Peter raised his hand politely but kept silent.

"Yes, Peter," Grandma said, acknowledging him.

"Can I just say one thing? You don't have to convince anybody to vote for you, Matthew. You're already a great guy—and a lot of people know it. You don't have to rely on a stupid old Grunge Worm song. You could write one that would be ten times better," he told Matthew. "And it would be true to what you stand for."

"Peter, I owe you an apology. I shouldn't have been irritated with you when we were raking leaves. You were right all along. A punk rocker who plays Grunge Worm songs and wears a skull-and-crossbones jacket is not who I really want to be. I really want to be a faithful disciple of Jesus Christ, and I want others to know it. So I was the one who was wrong, Peter. Will you forgive me?" Matthew asked sincerely.

"Of course!" Peter said without hesitation.

"So you're not worried about what your friends are going to say?" Katie asked.

"So-called friends, you mean." Peter reminded her.

She smiled, "That's right, so-called friends."

"We're your *true* friends, Matthew. And we're all the help you need," Peter went on. "I've got a great idea! You write the song, and Katie and I will sing backup."

"That's how Daniel and his friends did it, you know," Katie pointed out. "They stuck together and followed Heavenly Father. And everything worked out, because God was with them."

"You know, I've been thinking a lot about Shadrach, Meshach, and Abed-nego," Matthew said. "When they were about to be put in the fiery furnace, they declared to the king that God could deliver them if it was His will. And then they said these words: '*But if not*, be it known unto thee, O king, that we will not serve thy gods, nor worship the golden image which thou hast set up.' Of course, I want to win the election. *But if not*, I will know I have been true to what I believe, and that counts for everything."

"You know how I said I didn't want anyone to know you were my brother?" Peter asked, smiling from ear to ear. "Well, erase that, bro. I want everyone to know we're related! Now, let's write in our journals quickly and then get started on that song!"

"Just one more thing before we write." Matthew studied the painting again, and then looked to Grandma with a twinkle in his eye.

"Grandma, even though he's older than I am, did you paint Daniel to look like me?"

"Well, maybe I was influenced just a little." She grinned sheepishly. "But more important than *looking* like Daniel, you have chosen to *act* like Daniel, and that's what matters most. Truth be told, Matthew, I painted the man I know you can become."

Strengthened by the example of Daniel, Matthew began his journal entry with these words:

"Today, I made an important choice,
a choice I intend to live by my whole life through.
Today, I chose whom I will serve.
And as for me, I will serve the Lord."

About the Authors

Alice W. Johnson, a published author and composer, is a featured speaker for youth groups, adult firesides, and women's seminars. After receiving a B.A. in economics from Brigham Young University and serving a mission to Taiwan, Alice was an executive in a worldwide strategy consulting company, and then in a leadership training firm. She is now a homemaker living in Eagle, Idaho, with her husband, Paul, and their four young children.

Allison H. Warner gained her early experience living with her family in countries around the world. Returning to the United States as a young woman, she began her vocation as an actress and writer, developing and performing in such productions as *The Farley Family Reunion*. She and her husband, David, reside in Provo, Utah, where they are raising two active boys.

About the Illustrator

Casey Nelson grew up the oldest of eight children in a Navy family, so she moved quite often during her childhood. Graduating with a degree in illustration, she taught figure drawing in the illustration department at Brigham Young University, worked as an artist for video games, and performed in an improvisational comedy troupe. Casey is employed by the Walt Disney Company as a cinematic artist for their video games.